Unfolding : The Hidden Pulse

Whispers to Self in A world Unheard

Tejaswani Upadhyay

Made with ❤ on the BookLeaf Publishing Platform
www.bookleafpub.in
www.bookleafpub.com

Dedication

This is for you—the silent warriors, for those who once felt lost but have now rediscovered themselves. Life happened, but those moments don't define you. Only you know who the true "you" is. People came and went, playing their parts in your story, but at the end of the day, remember: 'ups' always follow 'downs'. Every scar, every tear, and every sleepless night tells the tale of your resilience. You are not shaped by your past, but by the way you rise from it.

Keep moving forward, for your journey is far from finished. Each step you take is a triumph, and each challenge you face is an opportunity to grow. You are stronger than you realize, and there is so much more ahead for you.

This book is dedicated to those whose hearts have bled but kept beating—a testament to your strength. Dear, you are not alone.

Love, Love!

Preface

When it seems that we are 'done with people', or I may quote 'done with the world', we often find ourselves in existential crisis. No one knows how to handle this journey full of hardships, still everyone finds their own unique way to make the journey worthy. There are times when there are real challenges that you face and can't address them to those around you, those people are close to you but you still choose to keep things to yourself, yes, because people don't understand and you are tired of giving explanations, but at the same time, also remember, never judge a person with a point of view of him being good 'or' bad, a person cannot be completely good 'or' completely bad but can be both good 'and' bad. And by keeping some things in mind, eventually we heal and the essence of who we are remains the same. This book is a reflection of that strength. You might not have all the answers, and you may still be searching, but remember, that's okay. Life is not about finding perfect answers, but about learning to embrace the journey, even when it's unclear.

As you will read, you know that you are not alone. And with every word, every sentence in this book, I hope that you find something that resonates with your own story.

Acknowledgements

Writing this book was a journey, and I thank God for the strength and guidance throughout. Also all this wouldn't have been possible without the love and support of so many wonderful people.

Thank you, daadu, my biggest motivation to read and write ever since I figured out life isn't just about milk and naps . To my cutie daadi, for your endless support and for bringing me love mixed with dry fruits every morning. Mumma, my pillar of strength thankyou for always having my back. And yes cheers to you , Papa, you always believed that I was going to do great!

Thanks, Deepanshu, for listening to my rants and laughing with me about the book cover and my life choices.

A heartfelt thanks to my long-distance friend for cheering me on, proofreading my book, and understanding my excitement when I finished the book.

To my ex-roommate Tanvi, thank you, 'sakhi', for wiping my tears every time I cried after writing a poem.

Thanks, Anmol and Pratham, for always being there and for those 3 a.m. walks and talks about 'AABA' and 'ABAB' rhyme schemes.

At last, a heartfelt thanks to you, dear reader, for being a part of my journey in sharing these feelings.

ROTTEN

She cried and said,
"Oh dear!
please save me from these tears"..
And continued,
"I love you with all my heart
That's visible to the greater mass
But why can't you see it in my eyes
Which cry and dry in the middle of every night skies?"..
Taking a pause
She added,
"I've learnt from my mistakes
I've grown with you
But is it
What do you think is true?" ..
With a heavy heart, quavering she asked,
"My lord or what do I call you,
Whatever you think is not always true
If you loved me
Then why did you let me turn blue?
If you say that's right

It has always been the truth for me
But why can't you see
That about you is all about me?"
Wiping off her tears she said,
"Only if I cry,
I won't complain to anyone but me
For that I've chosen to be
But being underneath your shade
Is what I crave
And the truth still remains forgotten
As your truth has been my truth
Because people say she is badly rotten"
And with these last words she died-alive forever..

REAR

Scared to be alone
Scared to be near someone
Shivering constantly
And a hope? there's none..
These thoughts consumed her
They had eaten her as a whole
That nothing seemed good
Because they made her think of herself as an empty hole.
The blue sky did not seem the same
The birds chirp appeared irritating,
And people near her
Said that she was faking..
Her journal, her voice said,
"It's not your fault dear
It's all me
I was not that clear..
But please don't sit next to me
And make promises
If you can't see deep
What's going on in my premises..

I beg everyone reading this
If you need anything
I'll still give my best
But now,
I really don't expect
It's not your fault dear
It's all me
I was not that clear..
And if I were that clear
What would be the difference
Cause you know you can't see
What's going on in the rear.."

CEILING

"I am ready to do everything
With all my heart
If it were still beating.
The tenderness I bought
Has lead to a place
Where even I am caught.
Staring at the ceiling
I wish you were here to hear
My breath - ailing.
Is there something I can do
For you to look at me
the same way
As I do?
If I could just hug you
So tight
That all my pain would go
As a leaving flight.
If I get a choice
Do or die
I would rather listen to the voice

That says "die".
But if there's you and me
I would rather
Choose you happily.
But haven't you done so much
For me
That we will just count on that
For another century?
But I am happy with all of this"
She said, talking to herself,
Staring at the ceiling
Crying within.

HELPLESS

Looking at her old bag, she said,
"I need that warmth
Just like grandma's knitted muffler had
When she gave it to me
I was so glad
That I danced to a merry song
And that happiness
Continued for long..
Those were the days
Where I just wished for a thing
And it was brought to me before even a blink..
But now I just need your warmth, beloved
Am I asking for too much?
Or you think
I do not love you that much?
It's a hidden part that's scared to come out
Because that's the only thing
Left with me in and out
Some words that remain unsaid
Come out as tears

At night on my bed.
I wish you could either
Unlove me my love
Cause then I would
Not hear when you say I don't love..
Or can we just sit under the sky
And appreciate the blue
And whatever about each of us is true?
Your love for me
And my love for you
Is the only thing
That saves me from turning blue..
So can you dance with me to a merry song
That I can say
And that happiness continued for long?.."

FORTY-WINKS

"Today..
I got up with a breathless me
That stared at the mirror
And made a fear trigger.
Tomorrow..
I am afraid of sleeping
As I see someone
Through the window, peeping..
I sleep in the hope
That I'll see you tomorrow
But these dreams take me far
Which leaves me in deep scars.
Yesterday..
I saw me in a dream
Wherein I mourned ,
For a body that I found
That was completely prolonged.."
And with a sigh she continued,
"Dreams..
That can never be

The truth that you are in..
Startle you within
And take away your forty-winks.."

RESENTMENT

Taking a sigh, she said,
"A hole in my heart
That let's in the dark air
Through which I cannot breath
Has destroyed all of my art..
A wind that is so cold
That makes me shiver
Through which I cannot see
If there's anything to hold..
A haunted past
That wakes me up at midnight
Takes my breath
As I cannot get past..
A chilling present
That has a hopeless behavior
Makes me cry
And fills my heart with resentment..
A window that's left open
With the golden glasses
Has pierced my legs

Due to glasses broken..
A hope if there's left
I cannot see, all i feel,
Is a weird feeling in the chest.."

GUILT TRIP

With the breezes passing by,
She stood there still
Looking at the sky thoughts ran through
And she took a sigh,
Remembering the past, a voice inside soft but sharp,
Told tales of wrong, and left its mark..
Taking a deep breath in,
She wanted to escape,
But the past, a ghost she couldn't flee,
Wrapped and latched around her plea,
She tried to run, but it followed near,
Silently and gradually turned into fear..
As she walked, the whispers grew,
A weight on shoulders, pulling her through,
Each step she took, reminded her the past,
Moving forward eating her till the last..
As a shivering remain,
She took a step, unsure but bold,
Wishing to break, to leave it behind,
But guilt's a trip that clouds the mind,

With it she stumbles and falls,
But it stays with her through all.

14

PARADISE/DEMISE

Haunted by the past,
Clearly in the mind
But by the face
Everything was fine..
Keeping it together
Holding it within
All she wanted was
A warmth therein..
When she looked for a hope
There was none
But a lot of anxiety
To cope..
The present was harsh
The past was dark
The future was all she had left
But will she make it up to the mark?
She once wrote ,
"A calm mind alone paradise"
And now
"She is just waiting for her early demise"

Her heart is a haunted place to visit
And her mind is a lone wolf
That will eventually consume her in a bit..
She can neither escape
Nor can be saved
All she has left
Is a stupid voice that condemns her
For the past and haunts her
For all that's left..

LOSS

A wound so deep,
That each chill that arose was so steep,
Life was still but wept,
Seeing her melancholy deep and inept,
She lost herself, nowhere to be found,
And a noise echoed within, a hollow sound.
The memories, oh , those memories,
The memories were in the air,
Reminding her of times when life was unfair,
"You lost" said her life,
But she knew it was going to be alright.
She knew "eventually things fall back into place",
But she doubted herself, unable to face,
Not sharing or speaking to people was all she had left,
Because there was no one to listen to her, she felt bereft.
With loss came tears from eyes,
That once had a smile of shine,
Now said that she was "just fine",
Being brave within and without,
Not losing herself that dark night,

She knew that one day, this loss with time will fade to grey.

GRIEF

A silent ache, that only silence feeds,
That intense pain, which leaves back a stain,
But with that pain came out scars,
Tearing her body all apart,
Scars that no one could heal,
It was all so messed up that she couldn't deal,
It clinged to her shadow and did not leave,
And kept growing as a wool weaved,
Being tired of the world, all the memories whirled,
Memories so haunting,
And all the thoughts were so exhausting,
That in summertime, her body was frosting..
Her broken soul, made a deep hole,
Time moves on but the ache's there,
Wretched her soul in and out but no one cared..
But again, she got up and took a first crawl
Leaving behind and feeling it all
By packing her feelings around a wall..
She made pain her teacher and scars her creed,
And from that wall grew the strongest seed.

FEAR

There was a thief, behind the shadows,
That weaved self-doubt and fear crescendos,
She questioned herself over and over again,
But no answers came from the head voices then.
In that silence, her thoughts took her to a place,
That she wasn't able to face,
Fear crawled and took her with it,
Into deep darkness where doubts would fit,
Fear : the thief tried to drink her blood,
And outside there was a tear flood,
But words were still unsaid; feelings untold,
So now it was time for things to unfold,
She took a step forward,
And fear pulled her backward,
She angrily stared into fear's eyes,
And slowly that thief started telling everyone lies,
But not caring for the lies,
Her steps proceeded with strength,
For she knew, the shadow would eventually recede,
And fear's hold on her would defeat.

LONGING

Amidst the silence, she realized,
the quiet was where she belonged,
A place where broken dreams had no space,
and the longing no one could replace,
In that stillness, her heart could breathe,
Feelings that she bequeathed,
Her consciousness whispered to the emptiness,
but she could hear or see only darkness,
In that hush, she found her soul,
Piece by piece she picked and felt as whole,
Under the darkness, her own thoughts tried to flee,
But in the chaos, they found a spree,
A storm of emotions, no calm to be,
In that silence, she felt an ache,
But she told herself that finally it was time to wake,
In those whole pieces, her strength began to matter,
Holding onto herself after everything shattered,
And, through the storms she learned to just be,
In the chaos and no calm to be,
She learned to just be..

HEALING

Every tear she shed, her heart bled,
With those tears as dark as red,
The pain spread..
Through the wall cracks, the helplessness fled,
Taking her into the past, where words were unsaid..
In the quite reverberations of the past,
She felt a cumbersome of the unspoken,
with her own voice broken,
But in that silence, she heard a whisper,
Helping her seek the light,
However,
the darkness acted as a resistor,
Keeping those thoughts to herself,
She chose to dwell on her past self,
Moving forward, with every step,
Consoling herself, she was ready to fight,
The weight grew light,
Her soul, covered with grime,
Healing her within, one tear at a time.

HOPE

She heard a quiet whisper, "I'll be alright",
She made it through storms and held herself tight,
There was a new dawn that welcomed her,
With no shadows of memories that recurred,
Even in darkness, light peeped through the smallest hole,
And she knew it was all hope.
Her journey ahead, was now clear but unknown,
But strength was a quality that she had ingrown.
Hope become her friend forever,
A lesson that she would forget never,
It stood by her in every weather,
Her core, once heavy, now felt light,
That even the night moon felt bright,
After the bright night, again,
Hope bloomed like a flower,
That now her life had a fragrance every hour,
Like the winter morning dew,
Hope carved a path for dreams to renew.
She whispered again, "I'll find my way",
For faith was her friend each day.

BEYOND

Sitting at the corner she said,
"There is someone beyond me,
A person, who looks up to me,
A person, who cheers me,
A person, who consoles me,
A person, who cares for me,
But that person is the one who is hurt,
By the shadows around me,
By the times gone by,
By whatever lies ahead,
By the time being,
I remember the times
When that person was full of life,
The person glowed like a pink light,
But one green light took it all away,
No hands could grasp the fleeting thread,
The shadows stretched the silent grew,
And in the darkness, the unseen tears flew."
She got up and said,
"That voice is still alive,

And will bring things align.
Yet through this darkness,
A light will shine so flawless,
It will give a promise of warmth within me,
And once again,
I will be the person beyond me..
I will be the person beyond me.."

CHANGE

The direction of the winds changed,
Decluttering the clouds around the sun,
With each shift, she felt unstrung,
She knew the change had begun.
The past was present there,
The present sat next to her,
And the future peeped through a hole near,
A new horizon awaited her gaze,
A world full of colored maze,
She looked straight into the eyes of past,
And asked the present, "Tell me, this won't last?"
Present replies, "Time is vast",
"But I assure this all won't last",
She sighed with a relief,
Giving way to things she still believed.
The winds no longer howled with fear,
So she sang a song that she could hear,
The past no longer clung her tight,
For change had come and it felt right.

FORGIVENESS

In the vaults of her heart,
Anger still festered,
Medicining her wounds,
Considering them as her shield,
But second by second she let go piece by piece,
The sorrow of the stain,
The weight now was so heavy and unyielding,
That she finally fought, with her heart slowly pleading,
In the quiet, she gave her a voice call,
Saying "Forgive, for only then you'll stand tall",
With a sigh, she let go the anger,
And then there was nothing left to linger,
No links or ties to bind,
No bruises to claim,
For her soul was free,
And, she was no longer the same.
In forgiveness she found her poise,
That was so much away from the disturbing noise,
Which helped her heal her wounds,
And made her make her own tunes..

BELONGING

After walking thousands of miles with the pain,
Lightheartedly, she exclaimed,
"I am home",
The birds chirping, the sound of the white within
Gave a way for a blissful day to begin.
With each step she took,
She got herself into a nook,
With a coffee and a book,
She had a glowing look.
Time healed her,
and clear thoughts were less blur,
Her heart was as heavy as air,
No regrets, no burden to bear,
She breathed as a whole,
Healing the wounds that scared her soul,
The "worried old she" was gone,
And all there left was a new dawn to look upon.

EUPHORIA

In the quiet where darkness lives,
Light fades away and pain strives,
She walked through all,
After a huge fall,
But there was a moment of light,
Where the sun shone bright,
Taking away all the pain,
She felt a warmth, breaking the chain,
Her pain wrapped her around her sorrows,
Piercing her heart with arrows,
Still, she sought peace,
Covering herself with the left good memories like a
fleece,
But in her heart, a fire ignited,
With that, a spark of hope she invited,
The whispers of the past grew faint,
Colored her heart with yellow paint,
Welcoming the peace she once denied,
In the light of her strength, she finally thrived.

GROWTH

Sitting at the corner she said,
"There is someone beyond me,
A person, who looks up to me,
A person, who cheers me,
A person, who consoles me,
A person, who cares for me,
But that person is the one who is hurt,
By the shadows around me,
By the times gone by,
By whatever lies ahead,
By the time being,
I remember the times
When that person was full of life,
The person glowed like a pink light,
But one green light took it all away,
No hands could grasp the fleeting thread,
The shadows stretched the silent grew,
And in the darkness, the unseen tears flew."
She got up and said,
"That voice is still alive,

And will bring things align.
Yet through this darkness,
A light will shine so flawless,
It will give a promise of warmth within me,
And once again,
I will be the person beyond me..
I will be the person beyond me.."

FREEDOM

She spread her wings and flew far away,
Far away,
Beyond the reach of hostility that wouldn't sway,
From the haunting winds that did not give way,
No borders bound her then
As she did not look back again,
She explored the whites,
In the sky of free will, she could finally glide,
She was no longer a prisoner of her past,
Nor needed to hide her scars,
In the stillness of freedom, she found herself,
Accepting her journey and moving on to a new self,
She embraced the new beginning with an open heart,
Knowing that no one could tear her apart,
Taking a a relieved breath in,
She felt a grace within,
As there was something new to begin,
And with a smile,
She told herself "Everything is fine.."